LOOM KNITTING

With the All-n-One Loom

This book includes 11 unique loom knit projects, each with detailed instructions and photos to guide you along the way. It features the All-n-One Loom, an adjustable loom for circular single knit, flat panel single knit as well as small to large gauge double knit. There is an array of projects from beginner to advanced; no matter what your skill level, you will enjoy the journey with all 11 projects. Absolutely, the perfect challenge for everyone! Great techniques and stitches are incorporated into the patterns, and you will find little tutorials throughout. Enjoy the Chain Lace stitch, Twisted Stockinette, felting, cables, and lots more. We hope that you will be both inspired and excited to jump into Loom Knitting. Have fun!

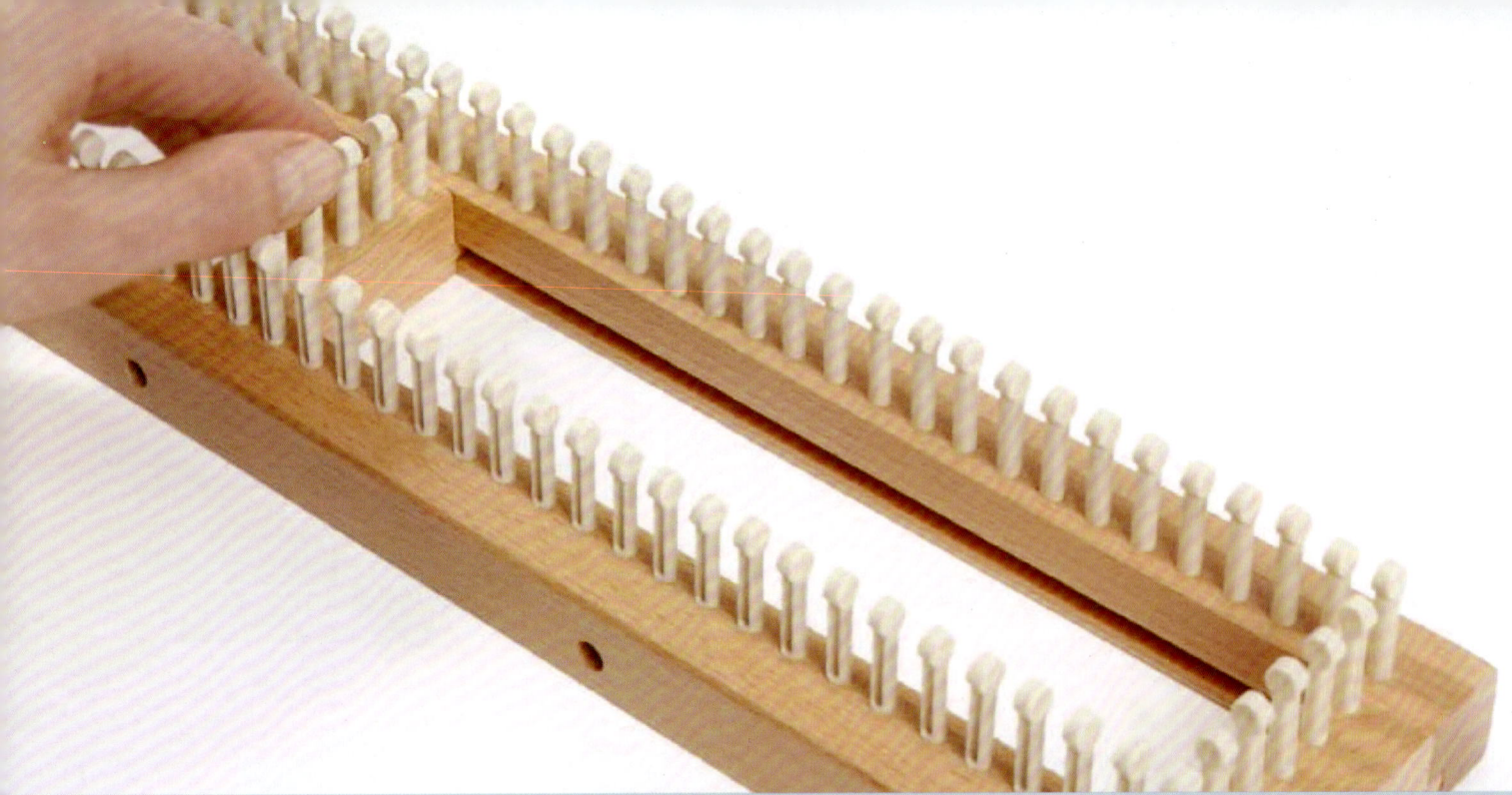

Patterns

Pattern Difficulty

BEGINNER •

INTERMEDIATE ••

ADVANCED •••

...Meet The Designers

This book is a collection of creations by some very talented pattern designers. They each bring unique designs that showcase the All-n-One Loom, and their passion for the art of loom knitting. We hope you will love all the wonderful new patterns and appreciate the talent that is expressed within.

• •

Isela Phelps is considered the leading expert in the loom knitting field. She is the author of various loom knitting publications, including the best seller Loom Knitting Primer. She has appeared on national television promoting loom knitting as an alternative way to create knitted fabric. Her tutorials and loom knitting videos have reached and helped millions in their quest to learn the craft. She maintains a blog at *purlingsprite.com* where she shares her passion for the fiber arts as well as her passion for staying active.

Felted Denise Bag, Slouchy Hat and Scarf, Cabin Wooly Socks, and Cabin Wooly Beanie and Scarf

Bethany Dailey has loved the art of loom knitting since 2005. She discovered that even with hand and wrist limitations, she was still able to successfully create lots of fibery goodies on her knitting looms. She soon began teaching locally, as well as online through her website, *GettinItPegged.com*. Bethany has participated in several loom knitting publications over the years and has recently released her debut book, *Loom Knitting for Little People*.

Market Hat, Chain Lace Daytimer, Scoots

Jennifer Stark has been working with yarn since 1996, when she learned to crochet. She picked up a set of knitting looms in 2007 and produced her first loom knitting design that same year. Jennifer shares her love for the fiber arts, along with some of her creative works at *guppylovesshark.wordpress.com*

Hadley, Ashley Shawl, Darby Wrap

Jacque Darragh has been loom knitting since 2008. She is creative in several areas, having written and recorded 5 albums of Christian music and is currently working towards a Master's degree in Fine Arts. Jacque has had a life-long yearning to knit or crochet, but was never able to produce beautiful pieces until she found the knitting board. Her favorite projects are afghans and throws with lots of color, and she's just expanded into Intarsia and Fair Isle knitting.

Cables and Lace Afghan

• •

Darby Wrap

Finished Size: 15" by 42"

Darby is a lively shoulder wrap with a subtle diamond texture. Worked in a vibrant yarn, Darby is spirited and adventurous. Be daring! Go Darby!

Materials

Loom: 60 peg, small gauge loom. All-n-One Loom was used in sample. Set up for single knitting.

Yarn: 4 skeins of aran weight yarn. Bernat Mosaic in Optimistic was used in the sample. (100% Acrylic/3.5 oz./209 yds)

Notions: 5 stitch markers or rubber O-rings (in a size that can fit over the pegs on the loom), knitting tool, tapestry needle, scissors, stitch holder, knitting counter, and a 2" button

Gauge: 8 stitches and 14 rows = 2 inches in Darby's Diamond Stitch Pattern. (Gauge is not critical for this project).

Pattern Notes

Darby is worked as a flat panel, in single knit. All knits are e-wrapped in this project. Darby's Diamond Stitch Pattern has a 10 stitch pattern repeat. The stitch markers will help with tracking the pattern repeats within each row. They are placed every tenth peg. Use the knitting row counter to help track the row sequences. Click the knitting counter at the end of each row. When the counter reaches 14, the diamond sequence is complete. Reset the counter and start the 14 row sequence again. The stitch holder comes in handy when working the twists. The twists can be worked without a stitch holder - the stitch holder just makes the process easier.

Instructions

Set the All-n-One for single knit using 60 pegs.

Place the stitch markers on pegs 10, 20, 30, 40, and 50. Working from left to right, cast on 60 pegs using the double e-wrap cast on method.

Border

Row 1: Knit all pegs.

Row 2: Purl all pegs.

Row 3: Knit all pegs.

Darby's Diamond Stitch Pattern

Row 1: P4, TW, P4; repeat to the end of the row.

Row 2: P4, K2, P4; repeat to the end of the row.

Row 3: P3, TW, TW, P3; repeat to the end of the row.

Row 4: P3, K4, P3; repeat to the end of the row.

Row 5: P2, TW, K2, TW, P2; repeat to the end of the row.

Row 6: P2, K6, P2; repeat to the end of the row.

Row 7: P1, TW, K4, TW, P1; repeat to the end of the row.

Row 8: P1, K8, P1; repeat to the end of the row.

Row 9: P2, TW, K2, TW, P2; repeat to the end of the row.

Row 10: P2, K6, P2; repeat to the end of the row.

Row 11: P3, TW, TW, P3; repeat to the end of the row.

Row 12: P3, K4, P3; repeat to the end of the row.

Row 13: P4, TW, P4; repeat to the end of the row.

Row 14: P4, K2, P4; repeat to the end of the row.

Repeat Rows 1-14 (diamond stitch pattern), until the fabric measures approximately 40 inches in length. (For the sample, the Darby Diamond Stitch pattern was worked 20 times).

Button-Hole

Knit pegs 1-5. Bind off pegs 6, 7, and 8, using the basic bind off method. Knit to the end of the row. Purl pegs 60-9.
Cast new stitches onto pegs 8, 7, and 6, using the double e-wrap cast on method. Purl pegs 5-1.

Repeat border (rows 1-3) once more.

Remove the wrap from the loom using the BBO method.

*Note: This stitch pattern creates diamonds on both sides of the fabric, but one side appears slightly different than the other. When attaching the button, keep in mind that the side that the button is attached will become the outside of the wrap.

Finishing

Sew the large button to the wrap, in line with the button-hole. To do this, lay the wrap flat. Find the button-hole at the end of the wrap.

It will be located at the bind off end, just above the first line of diamonds. Follow this line of diamonds down to the opposite end of the wrap. Sew the button to the wrap, centering it in the third diamond on the cast on end of the wrap. Darby sits loosely around the shoulders. If needed, the button placement can be changed to alter the way the wrap fits. You may also want to reinforce the edges of the button-hole with a simple blanket stitch, or whipstitch. Weave in all yarn ends. Lightly steam the wrap and gently block to shape. Wear Darby wrapped around the shoulders and buttoned in front. If preferred, the button-hole can be omitted and a shawl pin can be used to hold the wrap in place.

Darby Options

Try Darby's Diamond Stitch Pattern in other accessories. Increase the stitch count and make Darby into a shawl. Just cast on 100 stitches and follow the pattern until the fabric is the desired length. Suggested length for a shawl is about 60". For a neckwarmer, cast on 30 pegs and follow the pattern until the fabric measures about 20"; for a scarf, knit about 60".

Mix it up. Make it yours. Go Darby!

TW/Twist
(worked over 2 pegs)

Knit both pegs. Pick up the stitch on the left side and hold it, or place it on the stitch holder.

Move the stitch from the right side to the empty peg.

Place the held stitch on the empty peg.

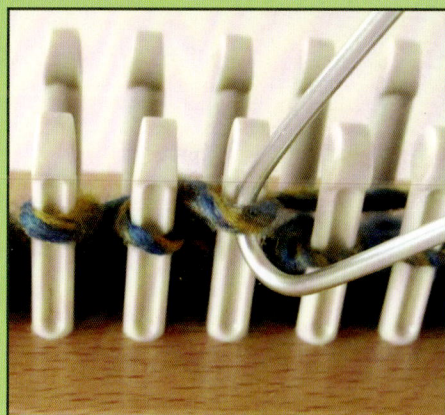

Market Hat

Measurements After Blocking: 8.25" from crown to edge of lace + 1.5" garter st brim. Circumference: 21.5"

This lovely hat is just the perfect item for those Saturday Market excursions. Wear it in the bucket style to help keep the sun out of your eyes while hunting for those flea market treasures, or wear pushed back as a slouchy hat, for a style full of charm.

Materials

Loom: 80 peg, small gauge loom. All-n-One Loom was used in sample. Set up to work single knit.

Yarn: Red Heart Soft: 100% acrylic, 204 yards per skein, 1 skein of Icy Pond and approx. 50 yards of Seafoam

Notions: Tapestry needle, knitting tool, 5.5 mm crochet hook, knitting pins for holding pieces together while stitching, and one stitch marker which has the ability to open.

Gauge: Garter Stitch: 4.5 sts x 12 rows per inch.
One lace pattern repeat: 4 sts x 8 rows per inch.

Pattern Notes

For the sample, all Knits (K) were worked as U-Stitches (Ust) throughout. Knit stitch and flat stitch can also be used if gauge is similar. This pattern uses the Chain Lace Stitch for creating the hat band section.

*Note: Refer to page 19. The Chain Lace Stitch in this case is worked by moving the first chain lace peg's loop over one, then E-wrapping the newly emptied peg 6 times WITHOUT knitting off. These are your "held" wraps. EW the next peg once and work 2 loops over 1. This will be the first chain of seven. Bring over each held wrap to this chain lace working peg and KO one at a time, for a total of six wraps that have been shifted and KO. The next peg's loop in line will be moved to the following peg, which will be worked as 2 loops over 1 in the first st of the next PK section.

Instructions

Set the All-n-One Loom to be worked in the round using 80 pegs.
CCO all 80 pegs.

Row 1: Knit row.

Row 2: Purl row.

Chain Lace Section: This section will serve to accommodate a knitted band. It will include a combination of CLS of 1, each consisting of a 7 st chain worked across 3 pegs, and sections of panel knits worked across 5 pegs by 9 rows.

- *pegs 1-5: PK 9 rows

- pegs 6-8: CLS (7). See note on previous page.

- repeat from * to last PK. Before last CLS, move loops from both pegs 78 and 80 to peg 79 and KO 3 loops over 1 on first st of CLS.

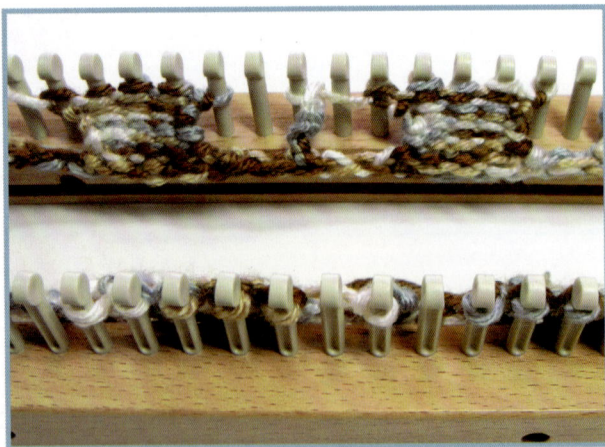

Chain Lace and Panel Knits

Cut working yarn at approx. 4".

CO new length of yarn and create the base rows for the crown sts:

Row 1: *K5, BtoF, K1, HHCO1(see photo), repeat from * to end of row.

Row 2: Purl all pegs.

BtoF= pull the straight connecting line that stretches from behind the CLS peg to the front of the peg.

HHCO, Half Hitch Cast On

Repeat the following 2 row pattern using all 80 pegs in the round for 54 rows:

Row 3: *YO, K2tog, K2…repeat from * to end of row.

Move the loop from peg 1 to peg 2.

Carry the WY across the front of the peg 1 and knit 2 loops over 1 on peg 2.

Knit the next 2 pegs in line.

Repeat.

Row 4: *K2tog, YO, P2…repeat from * to end of row.

Move the loop from peg 2 over to peg 1. Knit 2 loops over 1 on peg 1. Carry the WY across the front of peg 2.

Purl the next 2 pegs in line.

Repeat.

Work 3 rows in the following pattern: *K2, P2, repeat from * to end of row.

Bind off by gathering purl stitches and then knit stitches:

1. Leaving a tail long enough to wrap WY completely around all pegs with loops twice, cut yarn and thread on a yarn needle.

2. Place a removable st marker over the needle and let it rest on the yarn tail between the first and last pegs.

3. Thread the yarn needle through each of the purl sts in line from the last row, skipping all the knit sts. Release all the purl sts from their pegs and pull the yarn tail a bit.

4. Thread the yarn needle through each of the knit sts in line, then release them from their pegs.

5. Using the stitch marker as a starting point, gently pull all the slack from the purl st yarn tail section, until there is a hole that just two fingers can fit through. These will form a gathered top at the underneath layer of the crown of the hat.

6. Holding your two fingers in the opening of your gathered purls, begin gently pulling the end of the yarn tail until most of the slack has been removed from the knit sts, forming the outermost gathered section.

7. Remove your fingers and the st marker and pull the yarn tail until first the purl sts are closed tightly, and then the knit sts close completely.

8. Knot securely to the underside and weave all ends into work.

Hat Band

CCO 6 pegs of contrast colored yarn. Garter stitch a 20" panel (190 rows) by repeating the following 2 row pattern:

Row 1: S1, K5

Row 2: S1, P4, K1

BBO all sts, leaving a 6" yarn tail for seaming.

Weave band through chain lace stitch and stitch ends invisibly together. Weave in yarn tails to underside of band.

Before creating the brim, a good steam blocking over a round shape helps to bring out the lovely lace sts. Make sure what you are using as a form is close to the size needed for a final fit. Doing this before creating the brim will ensure that the brim is made to the exact size of the completed hat circumference.

Hat Brim

Leaving a 16" yarn tail, CCO 8 pegs of hat colored yarn, to be worked as a flat panel in single knit.

Rows 1-290 (approx. 21.5"):
Repeat the following 4 row pattern:

Row 1: S1, K7

Row 2: S1, P6, K1

Row 3: S1, K5...this will be your turning peg for this row. A st marker placed on this peg helps keep easy count as you work the rows.

Row 4: S1, P4, K1

BBO all pegs, leaving a yarn tail of a length that can wrap around the loom 1¼ times.

Pin brim evenly around bottom edge of hat.

Using your band CO yarn tail, stitch brim ends invisibly together. Weave in ends close to work.

Using your long BO yarn tail, stitch the brim invisibly into place on the base of the hat.

*Note: Measure your brim to your blocked hat section as it is worked, to be sure to make the exact length needed for your hat.

Chain Lace Daytimer

Finished Size: 12" x 12" without handles

Create this beautiful double layered carry-all purse featuring the special Chain Lace technique. The breezy nature of the Chain Lace overlay, combined with the strength of double knit makes this peek-a-boo color accessory the perfect item to brighten up your wardrobe.

Materials

Loom: All-n-One Loom used in sample. This tote bag is worked using single knit and double knit at 1cm spacing.

Yarn: : Naturally Caron Joy! #4 worsted weight, 70% acrylic, 30% rayon from bamboo, 138 yards per skein, 3 skeins in Sunset, 2 skeins in Cerise

Notions: Tapestry needle, knitting tool, 5.5 mm crochet hook, knitting pins for aid in seaming, bamboo oval purse handles (sample uses 8.5" x 5.5" by Purse-n-alize-it), large decorative button (sample uses 1 3/16 coconut button), 9.5" x 3.5" piece of plastic canvas for bottom support.

Gauge: Gauge is not essential for this project.

Instructions

Creating the Shell

This shell is started in single knit, and then changes to double knit. Set up loom with 1cm spacing. Using the shell colored yarn, CCO the 34 pegs in the center of the **front side** of the loom ONLY. You will have 7 empty pegs on each side of the CO pegs.

Rows 1-22 (2.5"): S1, K33

*Note: Sample uses the Ust for these Ks. A Ust wraps the working yarn around the front of peg in the shape of a "U" and knits off to form a quick Knit st.

Wrap the WY around the loom once and cut yarn at this point for seaming the handles later.

Change to double knit: DKCO all 48 pegs of the loom, using a length of waste yarn, as an anchor yarn, to hold CO sts for finishing later. KO 2 loops over 1 on the 34 pegs already worked.

Rows 23-66 (44 rows, 11"): DKS all sts.

BO 7 peg pair on each end (this will leave you with 34 double sts in the center of the loom):
Pull the loops of the 7 BO sts from the back pegs over to the pegs directly opposite them at the front. Work a BBO

loosely at the WY side, lifting 2 loops over 1. Do not cut WY!

Using approx. 18" length of the same colored yarn, BBO the other end pegs 2 loops over 1, working from the last peg inward, toward the knitting. Leave approx. 6" tails for seaming later.

Rows 67-82 (16 rows, 4"): DKS the remaining 34 sts.

Cut WY to approx. 4".

DKCO all the pegs, including the 14 previously BO, starting from one end and working across to the other. Use an anchor yarn to hold the sts for finishing later. Work the center 34 peg pairs; wrap the loom once again to be able to work all peg pairs.

Rows 83-126 (44 rows, 11"): DKS all sts.

BO 7 peg pairs on each end, in the same manner as before. Pull the remaining 34 back peg loops to the front pegs. KO 2 loops over 1 in the next row.

Rows 127-148 (22 rows, 2.5"): Work in single knit. S1, K33.

BO all pegs. Wrap the WY around the loom once and cut yarn at this point for seaming the handles later.

Using a crochet hook, BO all the DKCO sts and remove anchor yarns.

Seam the sides of the bag securely closed, working from the top of the bag toward the bottom. Hold the flat panel at the bottom of the bag against the newly seamed side, so that the seam is exactly at the center of the opening. Stitch this opening securely closed. The seams will form a "T" shape (see photo).

Using long tails saved for seaming the handles, wrap the top single knit sections over the handles to the point where the double knitting begins and stitch securely and evenly closed.

Weave in all ends and trim close to work.

Chain Lace Overlay

This Chain Lace Stitch is worked with a series of chains knit in multiples of six. Set up loom to work single knit. CCO 84 stitches. Work in the round.

Rows 1-8: *Row 1: EW all pegs.

Row 2: P all pegs.

Repeat from *

Row 9: Work one row of Chain Lace Stitch (See page 19)

Row 10: Work over a repeat of 4 pegs in the following method:

- *Peg 1: P

- Peg 2: Place the line of yarn traveling behind the peg from the previous row up and over the front of the peg. P this newly placed loop.

- Peg 3: P

- Peg 4: HHCO (see photo on page 10)

- Repeat from * to end of row.

Row 11: EW all pegs

Row 12: P all pegs

Row 13: Work 1 row of CLS. This row will work the chains on different pegs than were worked on row 9:

- *Peg 1: move loop to peg 2.

- Peg 2: EW and KO 6 times to create a chain.

Chain Lace Overlay

"T" Shape Seam

- **Peg 3:** move loop to peg 4, EW around peg 5 times (DO NOT KO!)
- **Peg 4:** EW once, knit off 2 loops over 1. Move the top EW from peg 3 to peg 4 and KO. Move the next EW from peg 3 to peg 4 and KO. Repeat process to KO all 5 EW's from peg 3. Peg 3 will now be empty.

Repeat from * until all pegs have been worked.

Row 14: Purl row using the same method as described in row 10, but begin with a HHCO for peg 1, and starting at peg 2, repeat the sequence from the top (at the *).

Row 15: EW all pegs

Row 16: P all pegs

Rows 17-20: repeat rows 9-12, this will be the 3rd row of CLS.

Rows 21-26: *Row 21: EW all pegs. Row 22: P all pegs. Repeat from *.

Repeat this entire pattern twice more, beginning with Row 9. At the final repeat, end the pattern with only 4 rows of garter stitch, rather than the previous 8 rows.

BBO pegs 1-49.

You will now begin to work as panel, using only pegs 50-84 (35 pegs total):

Panel Knit Rows 1-28 using the following 2 row pattern:

Row a: S1, EW34

Row b: S1, P33, EW1

BBO all pegs, making sure to work with a loose tension.

Securely stitch the panel knit BO directly across onto the opposite side of the CLS, leaving some stretch in the seam. Close the two side openings in the same manner that the bottom side openings of the bag were closed.

Knot securely, weave in yarn tails, and trim close to work.

Place your 3.5"x 10.5" piece of plastic canvas into the CLS overlay base.

Note: The sample's plastic canvas base piece also had rounded edges.

Slip the CLS overlay up onto the bag shell. Match the corners of the shell to the overlay and pin in place. Invisibly stitch the overlay onto the shell at the top edge of the base, working from the outside of the bag and only hooking through the outermost layer of the double knitting of the shell. This will secure the plastic canvas and create a border of garter stitch around the base of the bag.

Chain Lace Stitch - Row One
(worked over a repeat of 5 pegs)

*Peg 1: EW and knit off 6 times to create a chain. (After this first peg, all repeats for this step will work 2 loops over 1 on the first of the 6 EW's.)

Peg 2: move loop to peg 3, EW around peg 5 times (DO NOT KO!)

Peg 3: EW once, knit off 2 loops over 1. Move the top EW from peg 2 to peg 3 and KO. Move the next EW from peg 2 to peg 3 and KO. Repeat process to KO all 5 EW's from peg 2. Peg 2 will now be empty.

Peg 4: move loop to peg 5

Repeat from * until all pegs have been worked.

For this number of pegs, you will have one carried length of yarn between the end of the previous CLS and the beginning of the base row. Just make sure to adjust your tension so as to not cause your work to pucker where this yarn is carried up to the first peg in line. You can later tuck these extra lines behind the chain while assembling the overlay and shell pieces, if you prefer.

Note: Before working CLS on peg 83 (the last chain of the row), move the loops from both pegs 82 and 84 to peg 83 and knit the first chain as 3 over 1.

Pin the overlay in place at the top edge of the double knitting and directly below the single knitting of the shell. Invisibly stitch the overlay in place at the top edges of each of the garter stitch sections of the CLS, starting first with the lowest one and continuing around each one in turn, toward the top of the bag. Use the same manner of stitching as you did while securing the base, so that the stitches are not seen from the inside of the bag. Stuff something inside the bag to help both layers hold together evenly. Use your hand under the area you are stitching so that you can ensure everything is lining up correctly as you work.

When you are ready to secure the top edges of the shell and overlay together, a whipstitch or a decorative blanket stitch both work nicely around the entire top edge. The sample uses the overlay colored yarn with a blanket stitch. At the handles, first work across the outside of the bag to secure the overlay, then work the decorative stitch again with the contrasting color across the inside of the bag, under the handles. During this extra stitching across the inside of the bag, the button and button chain can be added directly at the center of the front and back, just below the handles.

Note: It helps to achieve even stitching to place a rectangular form into the base of the bag while securing in place. Keep double checking your work to make sure that everything is coming out evenly.

The button chain is created by stitching once through the place where the chain will come out from, just to the side of the center back, to form a small loop. A crochet hook is placed into this loop and a simple chain is worked using the WY and hook. Work to the length needed to wrap around your button of choice and back through the other side of the center back. The decorative stitching can be continued from this point at the inside of the bag.

Knot all ends; weave yarn tails into the inside of the double knitted shell, and trim close to work.

Ashley Shawl

Finished Size: Without border – 10" at the widest point by 65" in length. With border - 12" at the widest points by 65" in length. (Border rows were worked a total of 21 times for the sample.)

This beautiful, lightweight shawl is the perfect accessory to wear when the air is chilly. Give the wrap a lovely, feminine charm with the scalloped border included in this pattern. Or, leave the border off and create a wrap that is simply elegant. Either way, Ashley will add delightful warmth to any ensemble.

Materials

Loom: All-n-One Loom used in sample. Set up as knitting board with 1cm setting.

Yarn: 3 skeins of aran weight yarn. Sheep(ish) by Caron in Robin Egg(ish) was used in the sample (70% Acrylic, 30% Wool/3 oz./167 yds)

Notions: Knitting tool, tapestry needle, tape measure

Gauge: 10 sts and 18 rows = 4" in double knit, using Half Stockinette stitch. (Gauge is not critical for this project).

Pattern Notes

Ashley is worked in double knit, using the Half Stockinette stitch. The cast on for this wrap is a variation of the figure 8 cast on method. Shaping for the wrap and the border is achieved with gradual increases and decreases.

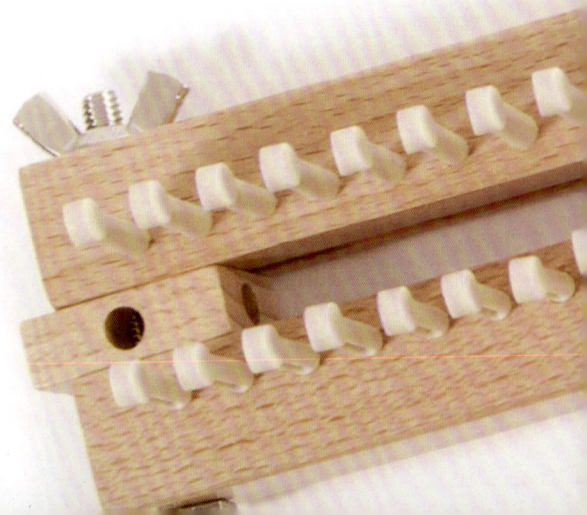

Modified Figure 8 Cast On

Starting on the left side, place a slip knot on the first peg of the lower board. Bring the WY to the 2nd peg on the upper board. Wrap the peg in a counter-clockwise direction.

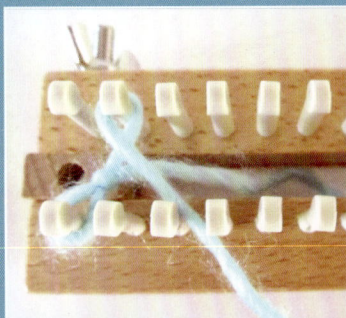

Take the WY down to the 3rd peg on the lower board. Wrap the peg in a clockwise direction.

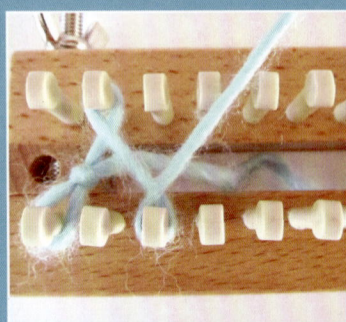

Continue working in this manner until the desired number of peg pairs (sts) have been wrapped.

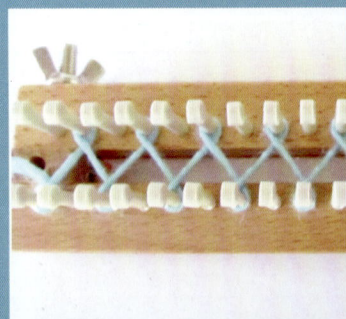

Complete the cast on by wrapping the knitting board in HS st, working from r-l. Knit the pegs that have 2 wraps on them.

Half Stockinette Stitch (HS st)

The HS st is worked on both sides of the knitting board, with the wraps travelling at a slant. One peg is skipped between each wrap. The skipped pegs will remain empty while working in HS st. Also, in this stitch pattern, one peg at the beginning of each row will serve as a 'turning peg' and will not be wrapped. When working from l-r, the 'turning peg' is the first peg on the lower board. When working from r-l, the 'turning peg' is the last wrapped peg on the upper board.

Wrapping in HS st, r-l: (WY will be at the last wrapped peg on the upper board) Take the WY down to the lower board and around the nearest wrapped peg. Take the WY back to the upper board and around the nearest wrapped peg. Continue working in this manner until all pegs have a second wrap on them, except the turning peg. Knit the pegs that have two wraps on them.

Wrapping in HS st, l-r: (WY will be at the first wrapped peg on the lower board) Take the WY to the upper board and around the nearest wrapped peg. Take the WY back down to the lower board and around the nearest wrapped peg. Continue working in this manner until all pegs have a second wrap on them, except the turning peg. Knit the pegs that have 2 wraps on them.

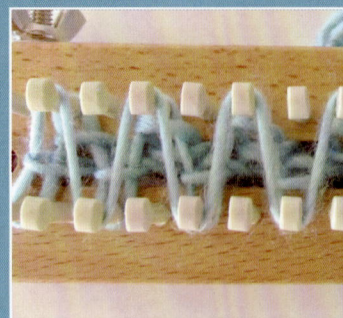

Work back and forth across the board in HS st until the knitted fabric reaches the desired length, or as directed in the pattern.

Instructions

Cast on 2 pairs of pegs with the modified figure 8 cast on method.

1st Side

The WY should be at the left side of the knitting board.

*Row 1: Work in HS st, l-r.

Row 2: Work in HS st, r-l.

Row 3: Work in HS st, l-r.

Increase by 1 pair of pegs: WY will be on right hand side of the work, resting at the last wrapped peg of the upper board. Take the WY to the lower board. Skip a peg and wrap the next peg in a clockwise direction. Take the WY to the upper board. Skip a peg and wrap the next peg in a counter clockwise direction.

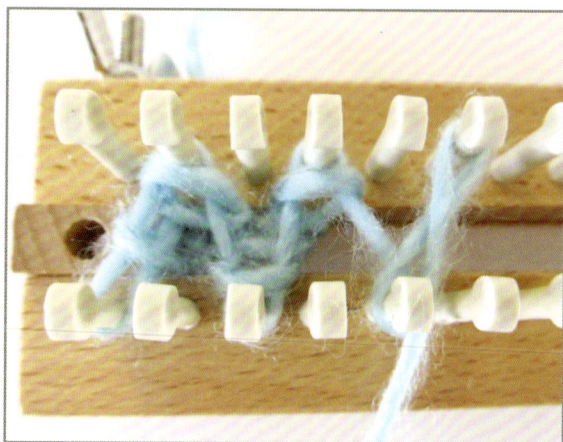

INCREASE

Row 4: Work in HS st, r-l.
Repeat from * until 24 pairs of pegs have been wrapped. The 1st Side will measure approximately 20" in length at this point.

Center

The WY should be at the left side of the knitting board. Work back and forth in HS st until the wrap reaches approximately 45" in length (measuring 1st Side and Center), or until wrap reaches the desired length, minus 20".

2nd Side

The WY should be at the left side of the knitting board.

**Decrease by 1 pair of pegs:
Decrease on the right hand side of the work. Pick up the last wrapped st of the upper board and move it to the left, above the nearest st. Pick up the last wrapped st of the lower board and move it to the left, above the nearest st.

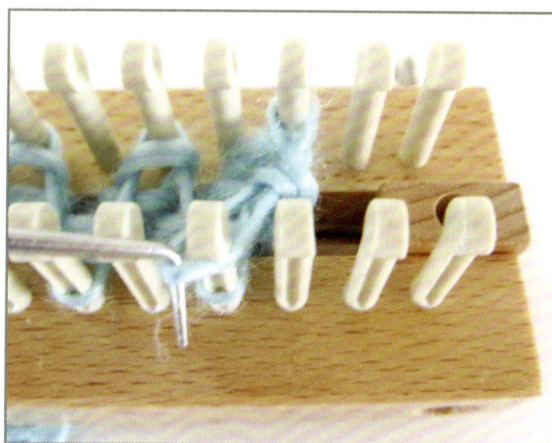

DECREASE

Row 1: Work in HS st, l-r. (Lift 2 loops over 1 on last peg of the upper and lower board.)

Row 2: Work in HS st, r-l.

Row 3: Work in HS st, l-r.

Row 4: Work in HS st, r-l.

Repeat from ** until only 2 sts are left on the knitting board; end with a row 4.

Bind off: Pick up the stitch on peg 4 of the upper board and move it forward to peg 3 of the lower board, above the stitch on this peg. With the knitting tool, pull the lower stitch up through the upper stitch and off of the peg. (This peg will now be empty.)

Move this stitch back to peg 2 of the upper board, above the stitch on this peg. With the knitting tool, pull the lower stitch up through the upper stitch and off of the peg. (This peg should also be empty.)

Move this stitch forward to peg 1 of the lower board, above the stitch on this peg. With the knitting tool, pull the lower stitch up through the upper stitch and off of the peg. Replace this stitch on the peg and gently pull on the WY to ease out any excess slack.

Cut the WY, leaving a 5" length. With the knitting tool, pull the yarn tail up through the last stitch. Remove the stitch from the peg and pull the yarn tail to tighten up and secure the last bound stitch.

Weave in all ends. Set the wrap aside until the border is ready. If the border will not be added, lightly steam the wrap and block gently.

Scalloped Border

Cast on 2 pairs of pegs with the modified figure 8 cast on method. Work a row in HS st, l-r. The WY should now be at the now wrapped peg on the upper board.

Row 1: Increase by 1 pair of pegs, then work in HS st, r-l.

Row 2: Work in HS st, l-r.
Repeat rows 1 and 2 until 6 pairs of pegs have been wrapped.

Row 3: Work in HS st, r-l.

Row 4: Work in HS st, l-r.

Row 5: Work in HS st, r-l.

Row 6: Decrease by 1 pair of pegs, then work in HS st, l-r. (Knit 2 sts over 1 on last peg of the upper and lower board.)

Row 7: Work in HS st, r-l.

Repeat rows 6 and 7 until only 3 pairs of pegs remain on the knitting board.

Row 8: Work in HS st, l-r.

Repeat rows 1-8 until the border reaches the desired length, minus 4 inches. Repeat rows 1-8 once more, this time decreasing until only 2 pairs of pegs remain on the knitting board. Work one more row in HS st, r-l. The WY should be on the left side of the knitting board.

Bind off in the same manner as for the Ashley wrap. Pin the border in place along the lower edge of the wrap. Seam the two pieces together. Weave in all ends. Lightly steam the wrap and block gently.

Cabin Wooly Beanie & Scarf

Finished Size: Hat fits a 22" circumference. Scarf measures 62" X 7"

One winter day I asked my son if he wanted a hat. He told me he wanted one but he didn't want one that looked like a girl hat. He wanted a manly hat that covered his ears and fit him just right. I agree with him, every man deserves a scarf and beanie set that fits him to perfection and has no frills, a manly beanie and scarf. Nothing too loose or too tight, the ribbing in this set provides the perfect fabric with the right amount of stretch for the hat and it provides a nice drape to the scarf.

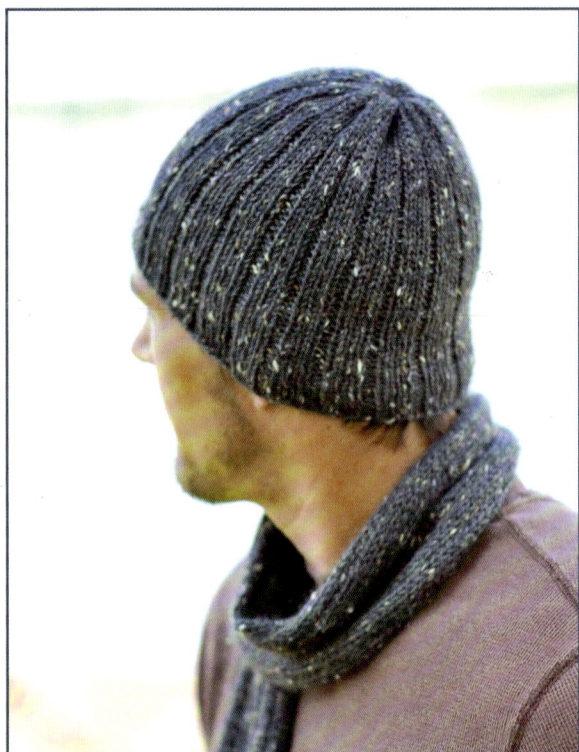

Materials

Loom: 48 peg small gauge loom. All-n-One Loom was used in sample.

Yarn: Approx: 650 yards of aran weight yarn. City Tweed Aran by Knit Picks in Obsidian was used in sample.

Notions: Knitting tool, tapestry needle

Gauge: 10 sts x 12 rows= 2" in Stockinette

Stitches: Knit stitch, Purl stitch

Instructions

Hat

Loom set up to work circular in single knit.

CCO 84 sts.

Rnd 1: *K3, P1; rep from * to the end of the round.

Next: Repeat Rnd 1 until piece measures 8 inches from CO edge or until desired length.

GBO. Weave ends in. Steam block.

GBO: Leave a 24" tail of yarn. Thread tapestry needle through the yarn tail. Take needle to the first peg and remove stitch and slide onto the yarn tail. Repeat the process with every stitch. Once all the stitches are on the yarn, pull gently on the yarn and cinch the top closed. Insert tapestry needle through and weave ends in.

SCARF

Loom set for single knit for a flat panel.

CCO 35 sts.

Row 1: *K3, P1; rep from * to last 3 sts, K3.

Rep Row 1 until piece measures 62" (or desired length).

BBO. Weave ends in and steam block.

Grafting for Cabin Wooly Socks (Toe)

Known also as the Kitchener stitch, it allows you to join live stitches seamlessly.

Prepare the stitches as follows:
Cut working yarn coming from the sock, leaving a 24" yarn tail and thread tapestry needle through the yarn. Position the first half of the stitches on one knitting needle, making sure to mount them properly. Place the remaining half of the stitches on the other knitting needle.

Step 1: Hold knitting needles parallel to each other, wrong side of the fabric together. Insert the tip of the tapestry needle through the first stitch on the front needle from r-l, as if to purl. Pull gently on the yarn. Leave stitch on the knitting needle.

Step 2: Insert yarn through the first stitch on the back needle from l-r. Pull gently on the yarn. Leave stitch on the knitting needle.

Step 3: Insert the tapestry needle through the first stitch on the front needle, as if to knit. Pull the yarn gently through, then slide the stitch off the knitting needle.

Step 4: Insert tapestry needle through the next stitch on the front needle, as if to purl, pull the yarn gently through. Leave the stitch on the knitting needle.

Step 5: Insert tapestry needle through the first stitch on the back needle, as if to purl. Pull the yarn gently through, then slide the stitch off the knitting needle.

Step 6: Insert tapestry needle through the next stitch on the back needle, as if to knit. Pull the yarn gently through. Leave the stitch on the knitting needle.

Repeat steps 3-6. Insert tapestry needle through the wrong side of the sock. Weave ends in.

Cabin Wooly Socks

Finished Size: Fits up to a 12" foot circumference. It will fit loose on a 9-10" foot circumference. It will be more fitted on men's 11-12" foot circumference.

Knit him a pair of socks that will keep him warm and dry during the winter months. The Cabin Wooly socks are knit in a nice worsted wool that will provide him with warmth and comfort. The stitch pattern is an intermediate level, providing the knitter with a more challenging design.

Materials

Loom: 48 peg small gauge loom. All-n-One Loom was used in sample.

Yarn: 300-350 yards of aran weight yarn. City Tweed Aran by Knit Picks in Toad was used in sample.

Notions: Knitting tool, tapestry needle, cable needle, 2 knitting needles size 6-US

Gauge: 10 sts x 12 rows= 2" in Stockinette

Stitches: Knit stitch, Purl stitch, Cable techniques

W&T=Wrap and turn (wrap the peg and knit in the opposite direction).
Rep=repeat

Instructions

CCO 48 sts, join to work in the rnd.

CUFF

Rnds 1-8: P1, [K2, P2] 3x, K2, P5, K3, P2, K3, P5, [K2, P2] 3x, K2, P1

LEG

Rnds 1-16: follow chart, page 35.
Leg Rnds 1-16: 3x more or until leg measures desired length.

HEEL

Cut yarn and re-attach at peg 37, peg 37 will be peg 1 from this point forward.

Knit from peg 1-23, W&T peg 24
Knit from peg 23-2, W&T peg 1
Knit from peg 1-22, W&T peg 23
Knit from peg 22-3, W&T peg 2
Knit from peg 3-21, W&T peg 22
Knit from peg 21-4, W&T peg 3
Knit from peg 4-20, W&T peg 21
Knit from peg 20-5, W&T peg 4
Knit from peg 5-19, W&T peg 20
Knit from peg 19-6, W&T peg 5
Knit from peg 6-18, W&T peg 19
Knit from peg 18-7, W&T peg 6
Knit from peg 7-19, pu wrap on peg 19 (treat wrap and loop on peg as one loop). W&T peg 20.
Knit from peg 19-6, pu wrap on peg 6 W&T peg 5.
Knit from peg 6-20, pu wrap on peg 20 (treat wrap and loop on peg as one loop). W&T peg 21.
Knit from peg 20-5, pu wrap on peg 5 (treat wrap and loop on peg as one loop). W&T peg 4.
Knit from peg 5-21, pu wrap on peg 20 (treat wrap and loop on peg as one loop). W&T peg 22.
Knit from peg 21-4, pu wrap on peg 4 (treat wrap and loop on peg as one loop). W&T peg 3.
Knit from peg 4-22, pu wrap on peg 22 (treat wrap and loop on peg as one loop). W&T peg 23.
Knit from peg 22-3, pu wrap on peg 3 (treat wrap and loop on peg as one loop). W&T peg 2.
Knit from peg 3-23, pu wrap on peg 23 (treat wrap and loop on peg as one loop). W&T peg 24.

Knit from peg 23-2, pu wrap on peg 2 (treat wrap and loop on peg as one loop). W&T peg 1.

SOLE

Rnd 1: K
Rep Rnd 1 until sole measures 2" less than desired length of foot.

TOE

Rep HEEL instructions.
Remove the stitches from the knitting loom and position them as follows on the two double pointed needles as follows:
Needle one: loops from pegs 1-24
Needle two: loops form peg 25-48
Graft the toes. (See page 31)

Weave ends in. Block lightly.

3-st RC (worked over 3 stitches)

Step 1: Place stitch from peg 1 onto cn and hold it to center of the knitting loom.
Step 2: Take working yarn in front of cable needle and knit pegs 2 and 3.
Step 3: Transfer these stitches to pegs 1 and 2 as follows: stitch from peg 2 to peg 1, stitch from peg 3 to peg 2.
Step 4: Place stitch from cn onto peg 3 and knit the stitch.

3-st LC (worked over 3 stitches)

Step 1: Take working yarn behind pegs 1 and 2 (you are skipping pegs 1 and 2).
Step 2: Knit peg 3; place stitch on cn.
Step 3: Take working yarn to the front of peg 1. Knit pegs 1, then peg 2.
Step 4: Transfer the stitches as follows: loop from peg 2 to peg 3, loop from peg 1 to peg 2
Step 5: Place stitch from remaining cn onto peg 1.

3-st RPC (worked over 3 stitches)

Step 1: Place stitch from peg 1 onto cn and hold it to center of the knitting loom.
Step 2: Take working yarn in front of cable needle and knit pegs 2 and 3.
Step 3: Transfer these stitches to pegs 1 and 2 as follows: stitch from peg 2 to peg 1, stitch from peg 3 to peg 2.
Step 4: Place stitch from cn onto peg 3 and purl the stitch.

3-st LPC (worked over 3 stitches)

Step 1: Take working yarn behind pegs 1 and 2 (you are skipping pegs 1 and 2).
Step 2: Purl peg 3; place stitch on cn.
Step 3: Take working yarn to the front of peg 1. Knit pegs 1 and 2.
Step 4: Transfer the stitches as follows: loop from peg 2 to peg 3, loop from peg 1 to peg 2
Step 5: Place stitch from cn onto peg 1.

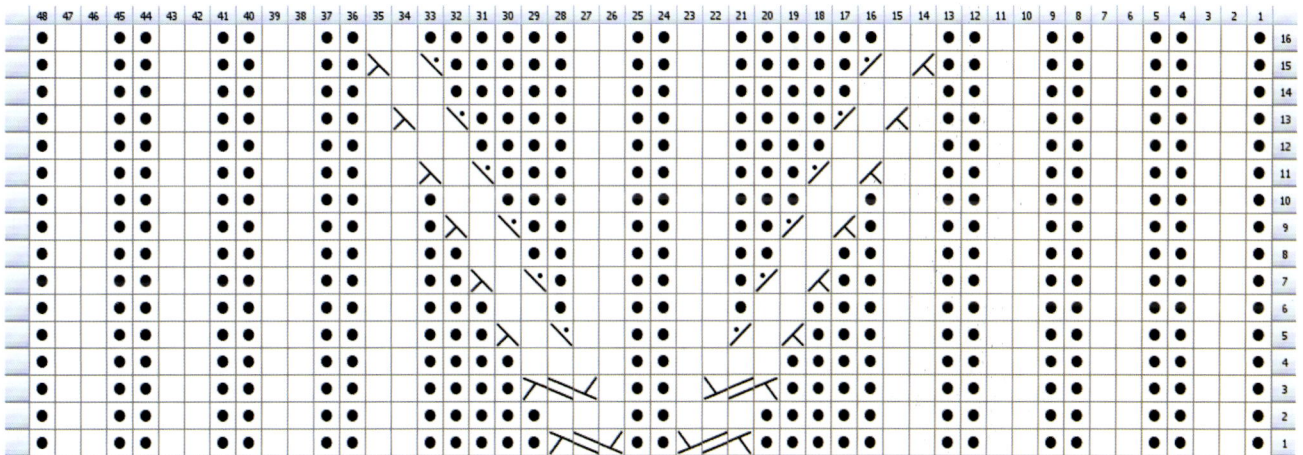

Chart columns (left to right): 48, 47, 46, 45, 44, 43, 42, 41, 40, 39, 38, 37, 36, 35, 34, 33, 32, 31, 30, 29, 28, 27, 26, 25, 24, 23, 22, 21, 20, 19, 18, 17, 16, 15, 14, 13, 12, 11, 10, 9, 8, 7, 6, 5, 4, 3, 2, 1

Chart rows (bottom to top): 1 through 16

Legend:

Symbol	Name	
•	Purl	
☐	Knit	
◪	3-st LC	(Left Cable)
◪	3-st RC	(Right Cable)
◪	3-st RPC	(Purl Left Cable)
◪	3-st LPC	(Purl Right Cable)

Slouchy Hat & Scarf

Finished Size: Scarf measures approx 32" X 5".
Slouchy hat: Brim area is approx 18" in circumference.

The inspiration for this set was born with the luxurious rich color of the yarn. It's rich turquoise color reminds me of ocean waves on a bright sunny day. The stitch pattern flows through the fabric to emulate the waves caressing the white sands.

Materials

Loom: 80 peg small gauge loom. All-n-One Loom was used in sample set with 5 peg sliders.

Yarn: Approx: 650 yards of worsted weight yarn. Vickie Howell Stitch. Rock. Love Sheep(ish) in Turquoise(ish) was used in sample.

Notions: Knitting tool, tapestry needle

Gauge: 8.5 sts x 11 rows= 2 inches in Stockinette

Stitches: Knit stitch, Purl stitch, Yarn Over

Pattern Notes

sl1-k2tog-psso: slip one, knit two stitches together, pass over slipped stitch.

ssk: slip, slip, knit.

M1L: Make 1 stitch. An increase of 1 stitch, created by reaching for the horizontal strand of yarn between two of the pegs. With the knitting tool, twist the horizontal strand into an e-wrap and place it on the empty peg where you want the increase to appear.

Edge (5 rows)

Next row: P6, yo, P2tog, P14, P2tog, yo, P6

Next row: K

Next row: P

Next row: K

BO

HAT

CCO 60 sts working in the round.

Rnd 1-8: *K2, P2; rep from * to the end of rnd.

Rnd 9: *K3, M1L; rep from * to the end of rnd. (80 sts)

Rnd 10: K to the end of rnd.

Body of Hat:

Rnds 1, 3, 5: *P2, K3; rep from * to the end of rnd.

Rnd 2: *P2, yo, sl1-K2tog-psso, yo; rep from * to the end of rnd.

Rnd 4: *P2, K, yo, ssk; rep from * to the end of rnd.

Rnd 6: *P2, K3; rep from * to the end of rnd.

Instructions

SCARF

CCO 30 sts in single knit.

Edge (5 rows)

Rows 1, 3, 5: K

Rows 2, 4: P

Body of Scarf:

Row 1, 3, 5: P6, [K3, P2] 4x, P4

Row 2: K4, [P2, yo, sl1-K2tog-psso, yo] 4x, P2, K4

Row 4: K4, [P2, K1, yo, ssk]4x, P2, K4

Row 6: K4, [P2, K3] 4x, P2, K4

Rep Body Rows 1-6 until piece measures 30" from CO edge.

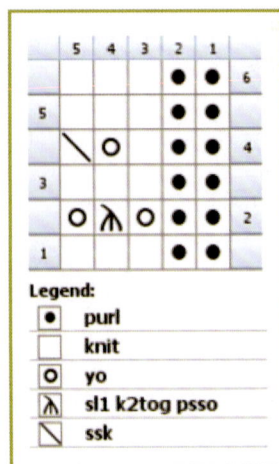

	5	4	3	2	1	
				●	●	6
5				●	●	
	\	O		●	●	4
3				●	●	
	O	⋏	O	●	●	2
1				●	●	

Legend:
●	purl
	knit
O	yo
⋏	sl1 k2tog psso
\	ssk

Breakdown of P2, yo, sl1-K2tog, psso, yo

Over 5 stitches, number the pegs as follows, working from r-l direction on the loom: (masking tape placed along loom works well for marking peg numbers. It can be easily removed when done). 5, 4, 3, 2, 1.

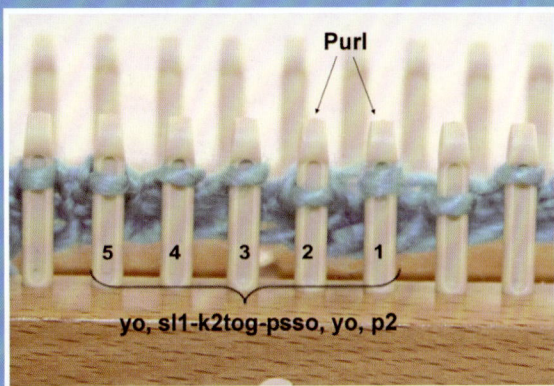

Step 1: Purl pegs 1 and 2.

Step 2: Move loop from peg 4 to peg 5.

Step 3: Move loop from peg 3 to peg 4.

Step 4: E-wrap peg 3.

Step 5: Skip peg 4 with yarn behind the peg.

Step 6: Knit peg 5, treating both loops on the peg as one loop.

Step 7: Move loop from peg 5 to peg 4. Lift the bottom loop off the peg.

Step 8: E-wrap peg.

Breakdown of P2, K1, yo, ssk.

Over 5 sts. Pegs are numbered as follows, work the row from r-l .
5, 4, 3, 2, 1

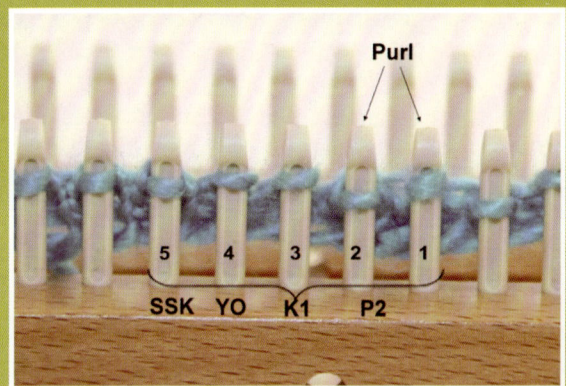

Step 1: Purl pegs 1 and 2.

Step 2: Knit peg 3.

Step 3: Remove loop from peg 5 and hold it.

Step 4: Remove loop from peg 4 and place it on peg 5. Place loop from Step 3 back on peg 5.

Step 5: E-wrap peg 4.

Step 6: Knit peg 5, treating both loops on the peg as one loop.

Little flower design on strap, not included in pattern.

Hadley

Finished Size: 4T (2T, 12 mos)

This sweet little toddler dress features a knit tank-top style bodice attached to a pretty fabric skirt. The bodice is worked in double knit Twisted Stockinette stitch. The skirt is created using basic sewing skills and then sewn to the bodice. If preferred, skip the sewing and make the Hadley bodice into a vest. Pair the vest with jeans or a cute skirt.

Materials

For Bodice of the Dress or the Vest

Loom: 30 peg small gauge knitting board. All-n-One Loom used in sample. Spacer set at the 1cm spacing.

Yarn: 2 skeins of a worsted weight yarn. Vanna's Choice in Dusty Purple was used in the dress sample and Vanna's Choice in Linen was used in the vest sample (100% Acrylic/3.5 oz./ 170 yds).

Notions: Knitting tool, tapestry needle, size H crochet hook, tape measure, 2 buttons (optional)

Gauge: 12 st and 18 rows = 4" in double knit twisted stockinette stitch.

Fabric Skirt Option Notions

Sewing machine, iron, scissors, 2 yds (1.5, 1) of cotton fabric, coordinating thread, sewing needle and pins.

Twisted Stockinette Stitch, TS st

Begin on the left side of the board. Place a slip knot on the 1st peg of the lower board. Take the WY up to the 1st peg on the upper board. Wrap the peg in a counterclockwise direction.

Bring the WY down to the 2nd peg on the lower board. Wrap this peg in a clockwise direction. Take the WY up to the 2nd peg on the upper board. Wrap this peg in a counterclockwise direction. Continue wrapping in this manner until the desired number of peg pairs have been wrapped once. When the last set of pegs has been wrapped once, bring the WY straight down to the last wrapped peg on the lower board and wrap this peg in a counterclockwise direction.

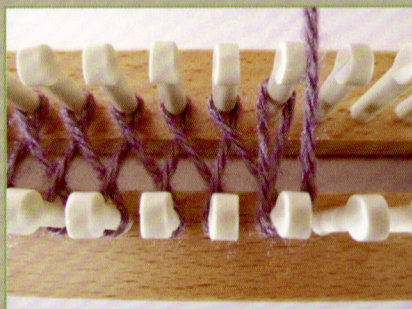

Take the WY back up to the last wrapped peg on the upper board. Wrap this peg. Bring the WY back down to the next peg on the lower board.

Wrap this peg in a counterclockwise direction. Work back across the knitting board, wrapping each set of pegs in a second 'figure 8'. When this step is complete, hook the lower wraps over the upper wraps.

Work back and forth across the board in TS st until the knitted fabric reaches the desired length, or as directed in the pattern.

Pattern Notes

The Hadley bodice (or vest) is worked in double knit, using the Twisted Stockinette stitch (aka fig. 8 st). The skirt is made from fabric using basic sewing skills. Follow the full pattern to make the dress. If making the vest only, the Instructions for the Hadley Skirt can be skipped.

Instructions

Hadley dress bodice or vest: (make 2)

Cast on 30 (28, 26) stitches.

If making the dress bodice: Work in TS st for 26 (22, 18) rows, or until the knit measures 6" (5", 4") in length.

If making the vest: Work in TS st for 50 (44, 38) rows, or until the knit measures 11" (10", 9") in length.

Decrease by two pairs of pegs: Pick up the 1st st on the lower board and move it to the right, above the wrap on this peg.

Repeat the process for the 1st st on the upper board. (1st pair of pegs decreased) Pick up the last st on the lower board and move it to the left, above the wrap on this peg. Repeat the process for the last stitch on the upper board (2nd pair of pegs decreased).

Work a row in TS st, knitting 2 sts over 1 on the end pegs.

Work a total of 6 (5, 4) decrease rows. There will be 18 sets of pegs left on the board when this step is complete.

*Note: If an even number of decrease rows were worked, WY will be on the left side of the knitting board. If an odd number of decrease rows were worked, WY will be on the right side of the knitting board. For the neckline, the peg where the WY is resting will be considered the 1st set of pegs (peg 1).

Neckline

Knit the first 4 sets of pegs (nearest to WY) in TS st.

For the next 10 sets of pegs: Move the wraps from the upper board across to the corresponding wraps on the lower board.

When this step is completed, the upper board should have 10 empty pegs in the center and the lower board will have 10 pegs in the center with 2 sts on each peg.

Bind off the center pegs: E-wrap the 5th and 6th peg on the lower board. Knit the bottom two sts over the top st on both pegs. Move the st from the 6th peg over to the 5th peg. Knit the bottom st over the top st. One st has now been bound off. Move the st from peg 5 over to peg 6 to close in the gap. E-wrap peg 7 and knit the lower two sts over the wrap. Move the st from the 7th peg over to the 6th peg. Knit off.

A second st has now been bound off. Continue working across the lower board until all 10 center pegs have been bound off. Place the last stitch (from peg 14) onto peg 15 of the lower board, above the st that is already on this peg.

Knit the next 4 sets of pegs (nearest to WY) in TS st. (Lift 2 loops over 1 on peg 15 of the lower board).

Straps

Work in TS st over the 4 sets of pegs nearest to the WY, (right side of the board for 4T and 12 mos; left side of the board for 2T), until the strap measures 3" (2.5", 2") in length - approx. 12 (10, 8) rows. Bind off all 4 sets of pegs for this strap in the same manner as for the neckline. Cut the WY, leaving about 10" in length to use later, when seaming. Finish binding off this strap by pulling the WY up through the last st on this side of the board. Remove the st from the peg and gently pull the WY to secure it.

Work in TS st, over the remaining 4 sets of pegs, until the second strap measures 3" (2.5", 2") in length. Bind this strap off like the first strap.

1st panel is now complete. Follow the preceding directions to make the 2nd panel.

Finishing

Pin both panels together. Seam them together at the sides, starting at the waistline (cast on edge) and stopping just before the underarm (decreases).

For the straps, seam the front and back pieces together at the top of the shoulder. Embellish each strap with the buttons, if desired.

Weave in all yarn tails and set the bodice aside until the skirt is completed.

If making the vest, a simple crocheted border can be worked around the bottom edge using the crochet hook, if desired. (In the sample vest, a row of single crochet was worked around the bottom edge). Once the finishing work is done, the vest is ready to be worn. If making the dress, follow the Instructions for the Hadley Skirt.

Before beginning the second strap, pick up the st nearest to the remaining 4 sets of pegs. (1st st of the neckline for 4T and 12 mos, last st of the neckline for 2T.) For the 4T and 12 mos size, place the st on the 4th peg of the lower board above the wrap on this peg. For the 2T size, place the st on the 15th peg of the upper board above the wrap on this peg.

Attach a new WY: Make a slip knot and place it on the 4th peg of the lower board (2T = 15th peg of the upper board), above both sts on this peg. (In the first round of this strap, knit two stitches over the slip knot for this peg).

Instructions for the Hadley Skirt

Sash: Cut a piece of fabric measuring 4.5" by 60.5" (2T: 4.5" by 55.5", 12 mos: 4" by 50.5"). Fold the fabric in half, lengthwise, with right sides facing each other. Sew along the open edge of the length using a ½" seam. Turn the newly created fabric tube right side out and press flat, with the seam at the bottom of the sash. Tip: The handle of a broomstick is very helpful in turning the fabric tube right side out.

Turn ¼" of fabric to the inside of the sash at each end and press with the iron. Sew each end of the sash closed. Clip any excess thread and set the sash aside for later.

Skirt: Cut a piece of fabric measuring 20" by 40" (2T: 18" by 38", 12 mos: 16" by 36"). The 20" (18", 16") side will make up the length of the skirt, and the 40" (38", 36") side will make up the width of the skirt.

Working along the bottom edge of the skirt, fold ½" of fabric to the wrong side and press it in place. Fold another ½" of fabric up and press in place.

Repeat this process along the top edge of the skirt, reducing the amount of fabric folded to ¼" each fold. Sew along the bottom edge of the skirt using a ½" seam. Sew along the top edge of the skirt using a ¼" seam. Sew a gathering stitch at the top edge of the skirt, just below the ¼" seam. (A gathering stitch is a long running stitch that can be pulled to gather fabric. It can be worked by hand, or with the sewing machine). Fold the skirt in half, width-wise, with right sides facing each other. Sew along the open edge of the width using a ½" seam. Stop just below the gathering threads. Don't sew over them. Press this seam open.

Pull the gathering threads to gather the top of the skirt until it is approximately 22" (20", 18") in circumference. Adjust the fabric so that the gathers are evenly spaced. Keep the skirt turned inside out and slip the knit bodice inside the skirt, straps pointing down toward the bottom of the skirt. Pin the skirt to the bodice.

Make sure to position the back seam of the skirt at the center of the back panel for the bodice. Try to keep the gathered fabric evenly spaced. Sew the bodice and skirt together using a ½" seam. It is best to work with the knitted fabric on top, away from the feed teeth on the sewing machine. It may also help to lift the presser foot to keep it from catching in the knitting. Alternatively, this step can be done by hand.

Finishing: Add the sash to the dress: Find the center of the sash and pin it to the front center of the dress, overlapping the seam at the waistline. Smooth the sash across the front of the dress and then pin it again at the side seams of the bodice. Sew the sash to the dress, stitching in a straight line along the side seams of the bodice. (This is best accomplished by hand with a needle and thread). After the sash is attached to the dress, remove the pins. The two ends of the sash can be tied at the back of the dress in a knot or a bow. Clip any excess threads on the dress that are left from the sewing process. Flower pin not included.

Felted Denise Bag

Finished Size: 12"w x 10"h x 2"d felted.
16" w x 20"h x 3"d unfelted.

A felted bag is the perfect accessory for any piece in your wardrobe. The felted fabric is thick providing protection for all its contents. The bag can be used to carry your loomy project or use it as day purse and carry everyday needs.

Materials

Loom: 75 peg small gauge loom. All-n-One Loom was used in sample, set up for single knitting.

Yarn: 660 yards of worsted weight untreated wool. Knit Picks Wool of the Andes worsted weight in Avocado (3 skeins), Orange (2 skeins), and Fairy Tale (1 skein).

Notions: Knitting tool, tapestry needle, knitting tool

Gauge: 9 sts x 10 rows= 2 inches

Yarn Color Abbreviations:
Avocado: MC (Main Color)
Orange: CC (Contrasting Color)
Fairy Tale: SCC (Secondary Contrasting Color)

Instructions

With MC, CCO 75 sts.

Row 1-100: EW knit (switch to CC yarn at row 60).

BO. Weave ends in.

Gusset: This narrow piece wraps around the 2 sides and bottom of bag.
With MC, CCO 20 sts

Row 1: EW knit

Rep row 1 until piece measures 56" in length.

BO. Weave ends in.

With CC, CCO 4 sts

Work a 60" length I-cord.

BO

I-cord Handle. Added to bag after felting.

With CC, CCO 4 sts
Work a 60" length I-cord.
BO

Step 1: Cast on 4 pegs. Working yarn (WY) is coming from the last peg. Take the WY and run it behind the pegs to the front of the first peg.

Step 2: Knit the pegs.

Step 3: Take WY behind the pegs and back to the front of peg 1.

Repeat steps 2 and 3. Tug gently on the cord every couple of inches to set the stitches. Then bind off with the basic bind off method.

Assembly

Use mattress stitch to sew the gusset to the front and back of the bag. This will create an invisible seam on the outside of bag.

Flowers

(Using SCC, Make 2 Large Flowers. Using SCC Make 1 Small Flower)

*Note: Small Petal and Large petal form the flower shape. If making the large flower, start with the small petal instructions and continue with the large petal instructions. The small flower uses the small petal instructions only.

Small Petal

CO 5 sts

Row 1: K1f&b, K4.

Row 2: K4, K1f&b, K1.

Row 3 and 4: K7.

Row 5: K1, K2tog, K4.

Row 6: K3, K2tog, K1.

[Rep Rows 1-6] 3x. If making Large Flower, do not cut yarn and continue with Large Petal instructions. If making Small Flower, stop here, cut yarn and go to Flower Assembly.

Large Petal

Rows 1 and 3: K1f&b, K to end

Rows 2 and 4: K to last 2sts, K1f&b, K1

Rows 5-8: K

Rows 9 and 11: K1, K2tog, K to end

k1f&b EXPLAINED

Knit 1 front and back

It is a way of adding a stitch. Also known as the bar increase, as it creates a horizontal bar when you create the extra stitch. To create this increase, you will need an empty peg to the right of the peg where you want the increase. Name the pegs as follows: Peg A (peg with loop on it) and Peg B (empty peg).

Step 1: Knit the stitch as usual on Peg A. Instead of popping the loop off the peg as you normally would when creating a knit stitch, place the newly formed loop on the adjacent empty peg (Peg B), leaving the original loop on Peg A and the new loop on Peg B.

Step 2: Wrap Peg A counterclockwise. Lift the bottom loop off the peg, leaving one loop on the peg.

Continue working the row.

[Rep rows 1-12] 2x

Cut yarn.

Assemble Flower

Thread tapestry needle with the same color as the flower. Use a running stitch along the straight edge of the long panel. Pull on the yarn tail to gather and form the knitted fabric into a flower shape, overlapping the petal so it looks like a rose. Tie the yarn tails together, knot to secure in place. Weave ends in.

Flowers will be felted with bag but attached to bag after the felting process is complete.

Felt the bag.

Attach flowers to right side at top of bag.

Handle Assembly

(Passed through bag after it has been assembled and felted)

Fold long I-cord in half, cut at the midpoint so you have two I-cords.

Mark the front of the bag: 1" from the top edge, 4" from the side. Insert a sharp pointy object through the felted bag. Insert I-cord handle through, coming from the front. Tie a small knot with the end of the I-cord that is hanging on the inside of the bag. Repeat the process to the back side of the bag.

FELTING INSTRUCTIONS

Set a top loader washer to the following: hot, small load. Place a teaspoon of Eucalan Wool-wash in the washer. Place bag, handle, and flowers inside a zippered pillow case. Throw pillow case inside the washer. Allow washer to start and go through the cycle. Stop the washer before the spin cycle begins. Take the bag out of the zippered pillow case and check for a felting process. If the bag has achieved a tight fabric and the desired dimensions, bag is ready. If bag still has not achieved desired dimensions, restart the wash cycle and repeat the process, again, making sure to remove the bag before it reaches the spin cycle.

Once the bag has achieved desired size, place the bag, handle and flowers between two towels, squeeze as much of the water out by simply patting it dry between the two towels. Do not twist the bag as this will create extra wrinkles.

Blocking the Bag: While the bag is wet, stuff it with a cardboard box that is covered with a plastic bag and allow the bag to dry completely, away from the sun. Shape the flowers and handle as they dry.

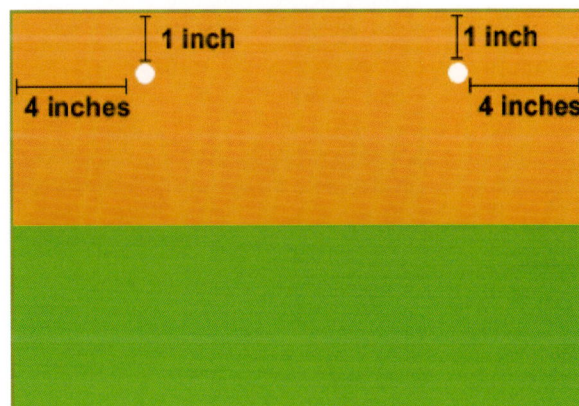

1 inch — 4 inches — 1 inch — 4 inches

Cables and Lace Afghan

Finished Size: Approximately 46" x 46" using bulky yarn

This is a soft and cozy afghan throw which has a luxurious look, but is actually quite simple to make over a weekend. This would make a great gift for any occasion from housewarming to wedding.

Materials

Loom: 48 peg, small gauge knitting board. All-n-One Loom (3cm setting) was used in sample.

Yarn: 1350 yards, bulky weight yarn. Lion Brand Jiffy (100% acrylic) in violet was used in sample (10 skeins), 135 yds per skein. Knit Picks Cadena wool/alpaca yarn is another option.

Notions: Knitting tool, tapestry needle, crochet hook

Stitches: Stockinette, Open Rib, Cable

You will knit 2 panels that will be seamed together. Each panel has a chart to guide you on the stitch pattern. Each panel is a bit different to make the seam more invisible.

Instructions

Panel One

Border Rows

Cast on 48 stitches in Stockinette. Place anchor yarn in heavy yarn.

Row 1-3: Knit in Open Rib stitch. (To begin Open Rib, move every other stitch on front board to the adjacent peg. You will have alternating 2 loops on one peg, and an empty peg).

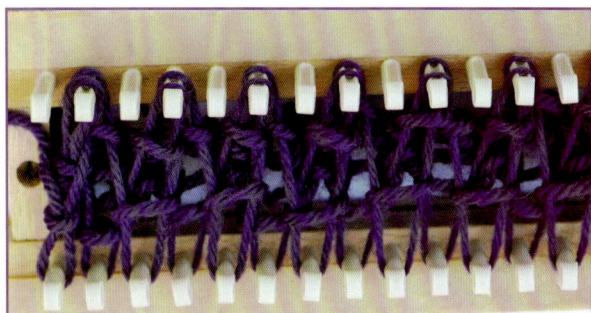

After row 3, move stitches out of Open Rib set up. Now there will be 1 loop on each peg.

*Note: You will be making your cables on the same side of the board as your open rib. Your cables will only be on that one side of the board. You will move loops for the lace on BOTH sides of the board. It may seem tricky, but once you've knit a few rows you'll catch on easily to the pattern.

For ease of keeping track of the stitches, put down masking tape and mark the number of pegs on both sides of the All-n-One. That way you easily know which stitch to move, and avoid having to use stitch markers.

Body of Panel One

Use Panel One chart below. Work rows 1-18.

Important note: The even numbered rows are all Stockinette stitch.

Repeat knitting Rows 3 -18 (18 is a Stockinette row), six times for the completed afghan to measure approximately 46" long. If a longer throw is desired, simply repeat the Row 3 - 18 row increments.

Now repeat the Border Rows 1-3.

Knit 1 row in Stockinette.

Bind off 1 over 2 stitches. Bind off also at the anchor yarn end with 1 over 2 stitches.

Row 1 and 3 Panel One Explained

Row 1: Move 10 to 11, 12 to 11 on BOTH sides of the loom (you'll have 3 loops on 11). This is the lace stitch.

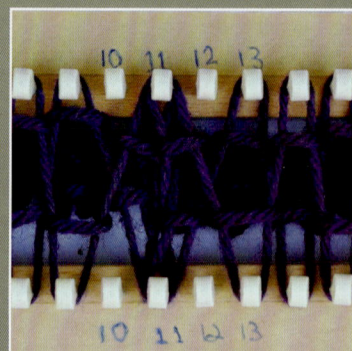

Pick up 22 and 23 with your fingers; move loop on 24 to peg 22; move loop on peg 25 to peg 23. Move loops which were on peg 22 to peg 24 and peg 23 to peg 25. You are making LEFT cables, which means when you've moved your loops, the stitches which were on the right are underneath, and the left-most stitches are on the top.

Pick up 26 and 27 with your fingers; move 28 to 26 and 29 to 27. Move loops which were on 26 to 28 and 27 to 29.

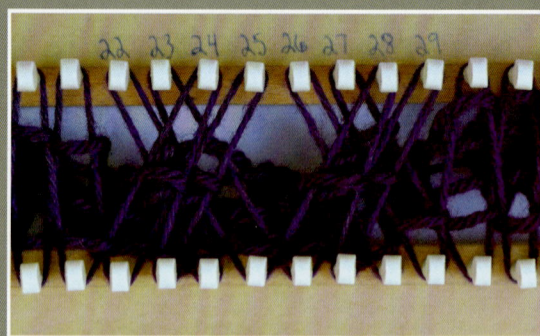

Move loop on peg 39 to peg 40 and loop on peg 41 to peg 40 on BOTH sides of the loom. You will have 3 loops on peg 40.

Now lay down a row of stockinette, and knit over. You will be knitting 3 over 1 on loops 11 and 40.

You will only have one loop on pegs 10, 12, 39 and 41.

These pegs will not be worked.

Row 3: Move 9 to 10, and 13 to 12 on BOTH sides of the loom (LACE). Pick up 26 and 27 with your fingers; move 24 to 26, 25 to 27. Place loops on your fingers which were on 26 to 24 and 27 to 25. Move 38 to 39, and 42 to 41. This is the RIGHT CABLE, which is only one set of cables to be moved. The left set of loops are underneath and the right-most set of loops are on top.

Panel One	LACE (BOTH boards)	Cable (One board)	LACE (BOTH boards)
Row 1	10→11, 12→11	Pick up loops on pegs 22 & 23 hold, move loops on 24 & 25 to pegs 22 & 23; replace loops 22 & 23 to pegs 24 & 25. Pickup 26 & 27, move loops on 28 & 29 to pegs 26 & 27; replace loops 26 & 27 to pegs 28 & 29. 2 LEFT CABLES	39→40, 41→40
Row 3	9→10, 13→12	Pick up loops on pegs 26 & 27, move loops on 24&25 to pegs 26 &27; replace 26 & 27 to 24 & 25. One center RIGHT cable.	38→39, 42→41
Row 5	8→9, 14→13	Same as row 1	37→38, 43→42
Row 7	7→8, 15→14	Same as row 3	36→37, 44→43
Row 9	6→7, 16→15	Same as row 1	35→36, 45→44
Row 11	7→8, 15→14	Same as row 3	36→37, 44→43
Row 13	8→9, 14→13	Same as row 1	37→38, 43→42
Row 15	9→10, 13→12	Same as row 3	38→39, 42→41
Row 17	10→11, 12→11	Same as row 1	39→40, 41→40

Panel Two	LACE (BOTH boards)	Cable (One board)	LACE (BOTH boards)
Row 1	8→9, 10→9	Pick up loops on pegs 20 & 21, move loops on 22 & 23 to pegs 20 & 21; replace loops 20 & 21 to pegs 22 & 23 . Pickup loops on 24 & 25, move loops on 26 & 27 to pegs 24 & 25; replace loops 24 & 25 to pegs 26 & 27. 2 LEFT CABLES	36→37, 40→39
Row 3	7→8, 11→10	Pick up loops on 24 & 25, move loops on 22&23 to pegs 24 &25; replace 24 & 25 to 22& 23. One center RIGHT cable.	36→37, 40→39
Row 5	6→7, 12→11	Same as row 1	35→36, 41→40
Row 7	5→6, 13→12	Same as row 3	34→35, 42→41
Row 9	4→5, 14→13	Same as row 1	33→34, 43→42
Row 11	5→6, 13→12	Same as row 3	34→35, 42→41
Row 13	6→7, 12→11	Same as row 1	35→36, 41→40
Row 15	7→8, 11→10	Same as row 3	36→37, 40→39
Row 17	8→9, 10→9	Same as row 1	37→38, 39→38

Panel Two

Step 1: Knit border rows.

Step 2: Use Panel 2 Chart. Work rows 1-18. This is made almost identical to panel one, but the loops are moved 2 pegs to the left.
Repeat rows 3-18, six times.

Step 3: Repeat the border rows.

Step 4: Knit 1 row in Stockinette. BO.

Finishing

Join panel one to panel two, making sure you match both sides with the cable stitch and the progressive patterns of the lace. Sew panels together with the invisible seam stitch.

Add 6" fringe if desired. Violet throw pictured used 4 strands of yarn together for each set of fringe which were cut at 14" resulting in approximately 6" length fringe.

Scoots

Reminiscent of the Peanut gang's footwear, these whimsical slippers are just the thing you need to scoot around the house during those relaxing days. Worked up in a flat panel with comfy garter stitch, these smart little footsies are a quick and simple project to whip up on your loom!

Materials

Loom: 69 peg, small gauge loom. All-n-One Loom used in sample. Set up for single knitting.

Yarn: Bernat Softee Chunky (#5 bulky weight): 100% acrylic, 108 yards per skein, 1 skein each of Teal (t), Grass (g), and Pumpkin (p)

Notions: Tapestry needle, knitting tool, 5.5 mm crochet hook, knitting pins for holding pieces together while stitching, 1 yard of ¼"-½" elastic, sewing needle and thread, large safety pin

Gauge: 3 sts x 8 rows per inch

Color pattern used in sample:
R1- 6: t, R7: g, R8: p, R9: p, R10: g, R11: t, R12: p, R13: g, R14: t, R15: p, R16: t, R17: g, R18: p, R19: p, R20: t
R21: g, R22: p, R23: t, R24: t, R25: p, R26: g, R27: t, R28: p, BO: p

Sizes: (S),M,(L) Instructions are for size M with (S) and (L) in parentheses.

SIZE Ladies 5-6 (S)
Length across bottom, from heel to toe: 9"
Width across bottom: 3.5"
Circumference around widest point: 20 ¼"
Opening Circumference: 5 ¼"

SIZE Ladies 7-8 (M)
Length across bottom, from heel to toe: 9.5"
Width across bottom: 4 ¼"
Circumference around widest point: 21 ¼"
Opening Circumference: 5 ½"

SIZE Ladies 9-10 (L)
Length across bottom, from heel to toe: 10 ¼"
Width across bottom: 4 ¾"
Circumference around widest point: 23"
Opening Circumference: 5 ¾"

Instructions

CCO (63 st), 66 st, (69 st), using color desired for top ribbing (sample=t) leaving an 18" yarn tail for stitching later (Helpful hint: 18" equals the length of the pegs of one side of the All-n-One loom).

Rows 1-6 (1"): Work in ribbing stitch by using the following 2 row pattern (K= Knit St or Ust):
row a: S1,*K1, P1, repeat from *
row b: S1,*P1, K1, repeat from *, knit last st

Wrap yarn around the loom once and cut at this point for seaming later.

Rows 7 - (18) 20 (22): Work in garter stitch by repeating the following 2 row pattern (K= EW):
row c: S1,K65
row d: S1, P64, K1

*See note below for helpful information regarding these rows!

Rows 21-28 (8 rows or 1"): Work the same as rows 7-20, but also add decreases to the garter stitch at the following rows: 21 and 22, 24 and 25, 27 and 28. (When creating sizes S and L, these row numbers will not match your pattern changes, so simply make sure to decrease evenly 6 times total).

Note: When a dec falls on a knit row: S1, move 2nd st in line to 3rd peg, move slipped st in to close gap, K2tog, knit remaining pegs. When a dec falls on a purl row: S1, move 2nd st in line to 3rd peg, move slipped st in to close gap, P2tog, purl remaining pegs except last, knit last peg.

Cut all colors except the BO color to 4". The BO color should be the same as the last color worked. Wrap the BO color (sample uses pumpkin) around the loom once and cut at that measurement.

Thread the BO tail onto a yarn needle and BO all but the last 20 center sts with the following method:

Thread the yarn needle down through the loop on the last peg worked on the opposite side of the loom.

Bring the yarn needle back to thread through the loop of the first peg.

Carry the needle back across the loom to thread down through the 2nd to the last peg's loop.

*Note: Have fun with your color combinations throughout the rest of the pattern. Some helpful hints for ease in working your stripes: Carry your new stripe color up the inside of your work, without trapping any of the other yarn strands as you do. Avoid carrying up yarn over more than 4 rows at a time. Avoid an excessive amount of trimmed yarn ends by using the yarns that are already on that starting side. Keep your knitting nice and even throughout by always working your EW's starting at the same side; Purls can be worked from either direction. Jot down your color combination as you go so that you can repeat it for your second slipper.

Bring the yarn needle back to the 2nd peg worked and thread it down through its loop.

Continue threading the yarn needle back and forth in a zig-zag direction across the loom, sewing down through each peg's loop in line, until there are only 20 center loops left unsewn.

Release the bound off loops and pull the BO tail until the sts are joined snugly together.

The last 20 loops will be bound off in a straight line, as is done for the top of a hat. Gather the stitches into an even circle about the size of a dime. This hole will then be seamlessly sewn together in a line even with the rest of the BO. When shaping this gathered toe section of the BO, it helps to open up the sides of the slipper so that they are lying flat and the BO is running up the center. Give the sides a little tug to help train your newly grafted BO sts to lie flat. Tie a small knot to the inside of the slipper and weave the yarn tail in securely before trimming.

With the sides of the slipper still lying flat, weave all the yarn tails, EXCEPT the 18" CO yarn tail and the longer ribbing yarn tail, neatly into the inside of the slipper. Trim close to work.

Using the CO yarn tail, stitch the back of the slipper neatly closed. Weave in this yarn tail and trim close to work.

To form your elastic casing, fold and pin the top edge of the ribbing down to the inside of the slipper, so that it sits just past bottom edge of the ribbing section. Using the longer ribbing yarn tail, stitch the folded section down along the bottom edge. Leave a small section open at the back to insert your elastic. Do not cut your yarn tail.

You can adjust the length of elastic so it is comfortable for your foot size.

Cut 2 pieces of elastic to about (13.5") 14" (14.75"). Attach the safety pin to one end and feed it through one side of the back opening. Work it through the entire elastic casing until it comes out the other side. Overlap the elastic by ¼" and attach together securely with sewing needle and thread.

Stitch the remaining section of the elastic casing closed with the remaining yarn tail. Work a small knot to secure, weave the yarn tails neatly into the inside of the slipper. Trim close to work.

Abbreviations

BO: bind off (removing stitches from the loom)

BBO: basic bind off method

CO: cast on

CCO: crochet cast on method

CLS: chain lace stitch, page 19

cn: cable needle

dec: decrease

dk: double knit (each st involves 2 pegs from opposite boards)

DKCO: double knit cast on

DKS: double knit stockinette or basic double knit st

EW: ewrap

Garter st: used in single knit so that both sides of piece are the same. Worked by alternating a K row and a P row.

GBO: Gather Bind Off- place the loops on sewing needle, gather, and pull through.

HHCO: half hitch cast on, page 10

HS st: half stockinette stitch (double knit), page 24

inc: increase

Invisible stitch: Used in double knit to create an invisible seam.

K: Knit

k1f&b: Knit into the front and back of the stitch. Used to create an extra stitch. page 48

K2tog: knit two sts together

KO: knit off or work the st

l-r: left to right

M1L: Make 1 (An increase of 1 stitch) page 37

P: Purl

P2tog: purl two sts together

Pu: pick up

PK: panel knit (single knit, flat panel)

peg pair: refers to a double knit st using 2 pegs on opposite boards.

R: row

rep: repeat

r-l: right to left

rnd: complete round in circular knitting .

S1: slip/skip one stitch

sl1: skip one peg with yarn behind the peg.

Sl1 to cn: slip one stitch onto the cable needle.

sl1-k2tog-psso: slip one, knit two stitches together, pass over slipped stitch.

ssk: slip, slip, knit

st: stitch   (sts): stitches

TS ST: Twisted Stockinette stitch (double knit), page 42

TW: twist (during a cable) or in special effect, page 7

Ust: U-stitch, a form of knit stitch with more stretch

WY: working yarn

W&T: Wrap and turn (wrap the peg and work in the opposite direction).

YO: yarn over

Production Team

Instructional Editor: Pat Novak
Project Editor: Kim Novak
Pattern Contributors: Isela Phelps, Bethany Dailey, Jennifer Stark, and Jacque Darragh
Photographers: Kim Novak, Isela Phelps
Technical Photographers: Jennifer Stark, Bethany Dailey, Isela Phelps
Graphic Designer: Felicia Cornish

For more patterns, videos, and looms visit www.knittingboard.com

KB Publishing | ISBN -978-0-9856769-0-2

Slouchy Hat

Scoots

Ashley Shawl